HELPING KIDS ALONG THE WAY!

The Social Skills Workbook

Z. ANDREW JATAU

The information provided in this workbook is designed to provide helpful recommendations for the reader and should not be used to replace the specialized training and judgment of a mental health professional. The reader should consult a qualified mental health provider in matters with respect to any symptoms requiring psychological attention. The publisher and author cannot be held responsible for the use of the information provided.

The Social Skills Workbook by Z. Andrew Jatau

Copyright © 2018 Z. Andrew Jatau
Cover Design by Z. Andrew Jatau
Illustrations by Alifstyle

Mylemarks LLC
Chesapeake, VA 23320
www.mylemarks.com

Printed in the United States of America

ISBN-13: 978-0-9964154-5-3

Table of Contents

Introduction

Social skills help to improve our interactions with those around us. By displaying positive social skills, children are better able to relate with peers and adults. This can lead to more and better relationships, increased confidence and self-esteem, and future success as adults. Learning and exhibiting appropriate social skills can be a challenge for some children. This workbook is a comprehensive tool designed to help parents and professionals teach these skills in a fun and engaging way.

The workbook begins by defining social skills and exploring its benefits. Next, readers are able to learn about social cues and different forms of verbal and non-verbal communication. Being able to effectively read social "clues" can improve a child's ability to relate to others and display empathic behavior. Chapter 3 focuses on the art of conversation. Readers will learn effective ways of starting, maintaining, and ending a conversation. They will learn the benefits of displaying active listening skills. The following chapter focuses on exploring ways to improve interactions with others. Readers will learn skills to enhance friendships and contribute positively as a member of a team. Chapter 5 teaches readers how to resolve conflict in a positive way. This includes learning healthy ways of coping with anger and learning to communicate assertively when upset. The workbook concludes with a chapter providing readers an opportunity to personalize the material learned and identify areas in which they may need to improve.

The Social Skills Workbook is filled with illustrations and activities designed to keep readers engaged as they learn about this essential topic. Discussion questions are also included after each activity to help prompt further exploration. Readers can take the knowledge gained from this resource and make it applicable in the home, school, and community.

CHAPTER 1

What are Social Skills?

What are Social Skills?

Social skills are the way that we behave and talk when we're around others. These things can have an impact on how other people feel about us and how they treat us.

People that display **Good** social skills usually have pleasant interactions with peers and adults. They are the type of people that others enjoy being around because they are kind and polite. This leads to them having more and longer lasting friendships. People with good social skills know how to have great conversations and show others that they are listening to them and are interested in what they have to say.

Someone with **Poor** social skills might have a hard time making and keeping friends. A lot of times, people don't enjoying being around them because they might feel annoyed, unheard, or disrespected. People with poor social skills have a hard time understanding how their actions impact others.

A good way to help tell the difference between good and poor social skills is to ask yourself this question:

"Will what I'm about to do or say make this person want to be around me or want to walk away?"

If it will make the person want to walk away, then it is likely a poor social skill and you probably shouldn't do or say it!

Why are Social Skills so important?

1. You'll feel happier and more confident!

Social skills help you interact positively with others. It's a good feeling knowing that other people enjoy having you around. Learning and practicing social skills can also improve your self-esteem by making you more confident when you are communicating with others.

2. You'll know how to make and keep friends!

If you have good social skills, then you'll know what it takes to be a good friend. Practicing these skills can increase the chances that more people will want to be your friend because they enjoy being around you.

3. You'll have better conversation skills!

Social skills can help you know how to start conversations and keep them going. People with good social skills *show* others that they are listening and are interested in what they have to say.

4. You'll recognize how others might be feeling or thinking!

Part of learning social skills is knowing how to guess how someone is feeling without them having to tell you! Being able to do that will help you better know what to say or do when you're around others.

5. You can express your feelings to others in a positive way!

People enjoy being around someone who knows how to express their anger or frustrations in a positive way. Social skills can show you how to better handle conflict and tell people how you are feeling without being rude or disrespectful.

6. You'll be successful later in life when you become an adult!

Yes! It's even important for adults to have good social skills too! When you become an adult, it will be useful to know how to interact with people in a positive way at home, work, and in the community. This is why it is good to start learning and practicing social skills now!

Good Social Skills

What are examples of **Good** social skills that you can think of?

What are behaviors that would make someone want to be around you?

Examples of Good Social Skills

👍 Sharing and taking turns when playing.

👍 Participating in activities and sharing your ideas.

👍 Being polite and friendly when interacting with other kids or adults.

👍 Covering your mouth when you cough or sneeze.

👍 Taking care of your hygiene so that it doesn't bother others around you.

👍 Respecting other people's personal space.

👍 Saying "please", "thank you", "excuse me", and "I'm sorry" when needed.

👍 Learning how to work things out when you disagree with someone.

👍 Showing good sportsmanship whether you win or lose.

👍 Being a good listener and *showing* others that you're listening to them.

👍 Knowing how to start a conversation and keep it going.

👍 Giving people encouragements and compliments to make them feel good.

👍 Using your manners when in the presence of others.

👍 Thinking about what you want to say before speaking.

👍 Expressing your feelings kindly and assertively even when you're mad.

👍 Making others feel welcomed and accepted.

👍 Being OK with someone telling you "no".

👍 Knowing how to work with others as a member of a team.

👍 Accepting helpful feedback from others.

👍 Caring about how your actions make other people feel.

How many of these did you have on your list?

Poor Social Skills

What are examples of **Poor** social skills that you can think of?

What are behaviors that would make someone not want to be around you?

Examples of Poor Social Skills

- Always wanting to go first during activities.
- Sulking or complaining when you don't get your way.
- Being rude and unfriendly when interacting with other kids or adults.
- Not covering your mouth when you cough, sneeze, or burp.
- Not caring about your hygiene and how it affects others.
- Getting into people's personal space and making them feel uncomfortable.
- Not saying "please", "thank you", "excuse me", and "I'm sorry" to others.
- Being mean whenever you disagree with someone.
- Being a "sore winner" or a "sore loser" after a competition.
- Making people feel like you're not listening to them when they're talking.
- Not knowing how to start a conversation and keep it going.
- Putting other people down or making them feel bad about themselves.
- Not using your manners when in the presence of others.
- Not thinking about what you want to say before speaking.
- Taking or touching other people's things without asking.
- Continuing annoying behavior even after someone asks you to stop.
- Throwing a fit when someone tells you "no".
- Not working well with others as a member of a team.
- Being disrespectful when someone tries to give you helpful feedback.
- Not caring about how your actions make other people feel.

How many of these did you have on your list?

Good vs. Poor Social Skills

Identify if the examples below describe Good or Poor social skills!

Kimberly and Sophie are sitting at the lunch table. Kimberly feels like she's about to sneeze. Instead of turning away and covering her mouth, she sneezes right into Sophie's lunch! Is Kimberly displaying Good or Poor social skills?

Why? _____

_____

How do you think it makes Sophie feel? _____

What do you think she'll say or do to Kimberly? _____

_____

11

Meredith is playing a video game with Trevor. Trevor wins every single time. Meredith turns to him and says, "Good game, Trevor! I'll try even harder to beat you next time!" Is Meredith displaying Good or Poor social skills?

☐ GOOD
☐ POOR

Why? _____

_____

How do you think it makes Trevor feel? _____

What do you think he'll say or do to Meredith? _____

_____

Hugo sees Colin playing with a brand-new toy robot. Hugo is jealous and really wants to play with it, so he walks up to Colin and grabs the toy right out of his hands! Is Hugo displaying Good or Poor social skills?

Why? _____

_____

How do you think it makes Colin feel? _____

What do you think he'll say or do to Hugo? _____

_____

DISCUSSION QUESTIONS

1. If you checked Poor for any of these, what can each person do instead to make it Good?

2. Have any of these situations ever happened to you? How did it make you feel?

YOUR EXPERIENCE

Look at the list of Good Social Skills on pg. 8! Which of these do *you* do?

Look at the list of Poor Social Skills on pg. 10! Which of these do *you* do?

Age Appropriate Behavior

Has anyone ever told you that you need to start "acting your age"? People usually say this when they think someone is acting immaturely or is using poor social skills. There are certain types of behaviors that people expect you to display depending on your age.

For example, a baby can get away with doing certain behaviors that a child and adult might not. When you become an adult, people will expect you to have learned all about good social skills and know to use them consistently.

B
A
B
Y

C
H
I
L
D

A
D
U
L
T

* can use the bathroom or throw up on themselves without anyone caring

* can stare at people without making them uncomfortable

* can do or say things without thinking

* doesn't have to share

* is allowed to cry and throw a tantrum when upset or hungry

* isn't expected to know when to be loud and when to be quiet

* is expected to start learning how to share with others

* can throw a tantrum when upset, but is expected to start learning how to cope

* is allowed to show poor social skills sometimes because they are still learning

* can act loud and silly with friends in public sometimes

* still learning how to communicate kindly and respectfully with peers and adults

* should have learned good social skills and use them most of the time

* should know how to handle their anger and disappointment without throwing a tantrum

* allowed to show silly behaviors sometimes when around friends and family

* expected to be kind and polite to others

* should know how to start a conversation with others and keep it going

Setting

Social skills expectations can change depending on the setting that you're in and who you are around. You might do or say certain things in front of your friends that you wouldn't do if an adult was nearby. For instance, if you burped in front of your friends, they might laugh and join in! Doing the same behavior in front of an adult or people you don't know well could be seen as rude or disrespectful. Certain settings have different expectations of social skills. In your classroom, you might be expected to talk quietly, but if you are at a park, you can be as loud as you want.

What are some other social skills that change depending on your setting?

Family

Every family has their own way of interacting with each other. In some families, being loud and interrupting each other is normal and is not seen as rude. There are some families where children are allowed to call their adult relatives by their first names, while other families encourage them to use "aunt" or "uncle".

What are the social skills expectations in your family?

Location

Social skills can also differ depending on which city, state, or country you live in. Most cultures have their own set of rules and expectations about how you should interact with others. For example, eye contact can be seen as a good social skill in some cultures, but there are many countries where looking an adult in the eye is seen as disrespectful. In some cultures, greeting a family member or friend with a kiss on the cheek is seen as a good social skill to have.

It's important to know what the expected social skills are in your community, culture, or country!

In your country...

What should you do or say when you first meet someone? _____

_____

What do you do or say if someone sneezes? _____

_____

What should you do if an adult is talking to you? _____

_____

Chapter Wrap-Up

There are many benefits to learning and showing good social skills. You'll feel happier and become more confident because you'll have a positive effect on people around you. This is true for kids, teens, and adults alike. Learning social skills while you're young can help you later in life as you interact with others. To increase your chances of people wanting to be around you, it is important to know the differences between good and poor social skills.

Social skills expectations can change sometimes depending on your age, setting, family, and location. What may be seen as a good social skill in one environment can be a poor social skill when you're in a different situation. At some point, someone will probably let you know what is acceptable behavior in most settings, but it is up to you to continue to remember and follow these guidelines. If you're ever not sure whether a behavior is OK or not, it is best to check in with a friend or trusted adult.

It may seem like a lot to learn, but this book will teach you ways to improve your interactions with peers and adults in your life. In the rest of this book you will learn about social "clues", having conversations, getting along with others, and handling conflict. Once you get through this workbook, you should have the knowledge to become a social skills master!

CHAPTER 2

Social Clues

What are Social Clues?

Social clues are hints that we send that let others know how we might be feeling or thinking in the moment. Social clues can be either **verbal** or **nonverbal**. Verbal means that the person is using their words to send you a message about what they think. Nonverbal means that they are sending these messages using parts of their body and they don't even have to say a thing.

Learning to read social clues is important because it lets you know how you should interact with others in the moment. If a person's social clues indicate that they are feeling angry, then it might not be the best time for you to tell them a funny joke. Instead, you could ask if there's anything you can do to help them feel better. This would probably get a better response from them.

Before interacting with others, you should ask yourself:

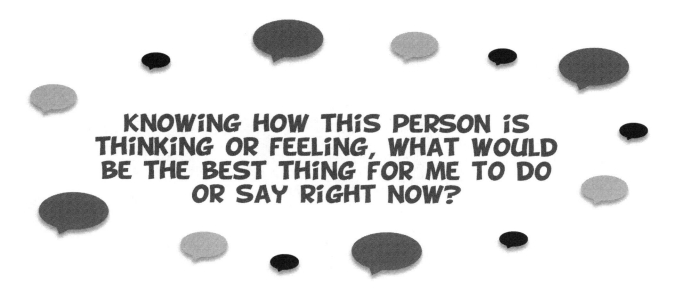

KNOWING HOW THIS PERSON IS THINKING OR FEELING, WHAT WOULD BE THE BEST THING FOR ME TO DO OR SAY RIGHT NOW?

Some people have a hard time reading other people's social clues, especially the nonverbal ones. This makes it hard for them to know what to do or say in certain situations. By learning the different types of social clues and practicing, you can become more in-tune with other people's feelings!

Social Clues

Imagine that you are a detective and it is your job to try to figure out what other people around you are feeling or thinking. What sort of things would you look for to help you figure that out?

You would be looking for **social clues**! Social clues include facial expression, body language, space, and voice tone/volume. The next few pages will teach you how you can use these clues to improve your social skills and interactions with others.

Facial Expression

A facial expression is when different parts of your face move and send a message about what you're thinking or how you are feeling. The combination of these moving parts can let others know if you're feeling sad, excited, annoyed, or any other feeling! The image below shows the different movements parts of your face can make to send messages.

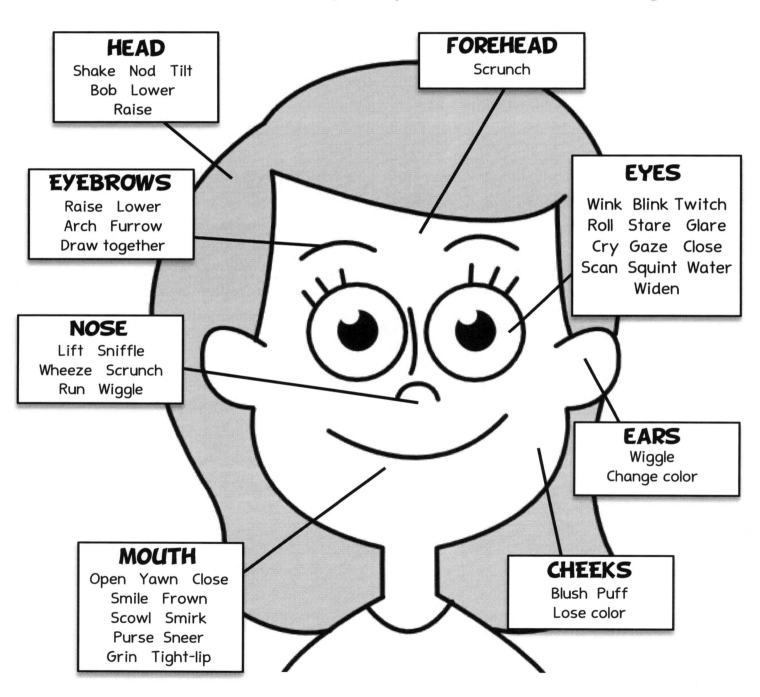

HEAD
Shake Nod Tilt
Bob Lower
Raise

FOREHEAD
Scrunch

EYEBROWS
Raise Lower
Arch Furrow
Draw together

EYES
Wink Blink Twitch
Roll Stare Glare
Cry Gaze Close
Scan Squint Water
Widen

NOSE
Lift Sniffle
Wheeze Scrunch
Run Wiggle

EARS
Wiggle
Change color

MOUTH
Open Yawn Close
Smile Frown
Scowl Smirk
Purse Sneer
Grin Tight-lip

CHEEKS
Blush Puff
Lose color

ACTIVITY

Facial Expressions

Match the facial expressions to the feeling you think it is describing!

1. Eyes wide open, wide smile

2. Frowning, watery eyes, sniffling nose

3. Yawning, heavy eye lids, head lowered

4. Smiling, eye contact

5. Smirk, head held high

6. Blushed cheeks, head down, looking away

7. Scrunched nose, tongue stuck out

8. Eyes wide open, mouth open, raised eyebrows

9. Scrunched eye brows, glaring eyes, scowl

EMBARRASSED

CONFIDENT

SAD

DISGUSTED

ANGRY

EXCITED

TIRED

SURPRISED

HAPPY

Answer Key

1.) excited 2.) sad 3.) tired 4.) happy 5.) confident 6.) embarrassed 7.) disgusted 8.) surprised 9.) angry

DISCUSSION QUESTIONS

1. Have you seen all of these facial expressions before?

2. What does your facial expression look like when you're experiencing any of these feelings?

Feelings Faces

Draw in the faces to match each feeling. Talk about the differences you notice in the facial expression of each person.

ANGRY

SCARED

SAD

HAPPY

DISCUSSION QUESTIONS

1. What were some of the major differences that you noticed in the faces?

2. Are there any feelings that you can think of that have similar facial expressions?

Body Language

It's not just your face that can send messages about your feelings. The way that you move the rest of your body parts can also let others know how you are feeling or thinking. Your body responds differently when you are feeling happy, sad, frightened, or any other emotion.

The way that you sit or stand is known as your **posture**. Sitting straight up in a chair might mean that you are paying attention and focused while slouching could mean that you are tired or bored. A **gesture** is when you use your head, hands, or body to send a message. Examples of gestures include thumbs up, fist pump, and waving.

What does this body language usually express?

Nail biting: _____

Rubbing hands together: _____

Clenching fists: _____

Thumbs up: _____

Head nodding: _____

Eye rubbing: _____

Shrugging shoulders: _____

High-fiving: _____

Fingers crossing: _____

Face and Body Clues

Looking at social clues, match the pictures with the feeling words that you think
fit how the character is feeling! (You can match more than one feeling word)

DISCUSSION QUESTIONS

1. Was it difficult for you to match up the feelings to the face and body clues?

2. Are there any other feelings that you think would fit any of these face and body clues?

YOUR EXPERIENCE

What do your social clues look like when you are experiencing any of the feelings below? Write descriptions of what your face and body look like in each box!

AFRAID

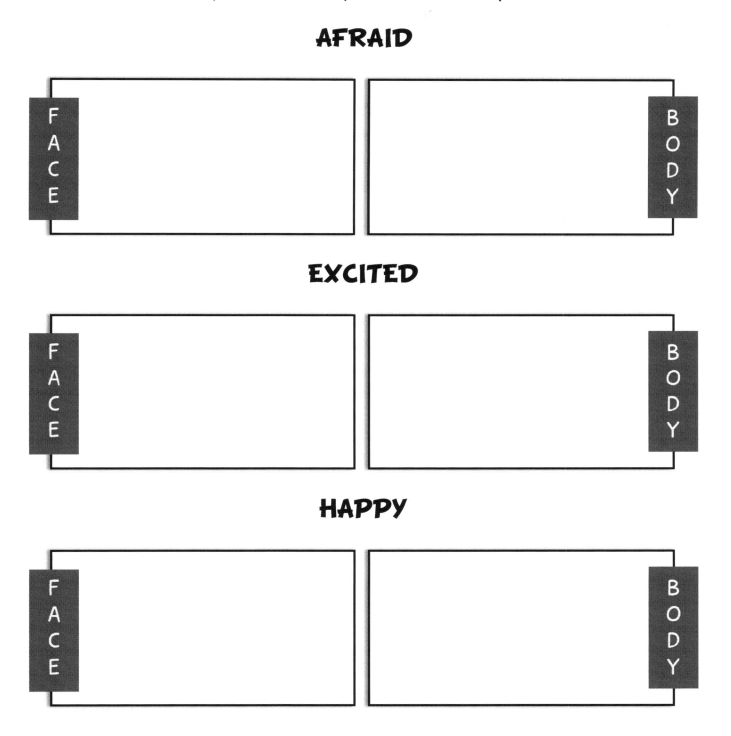

FACE		BODY

EXCITED

FACE		BODY

HAPPY

FACE		BODY

What about when you're feeling shy, annoyed, or bored?

Space

Space is how close or far away you are from another person. Most people feel uncomfortable whenever someone is too close to them. They feel that the person is invading their **personal space**. The more you know and like someone, the closer you may allow them to get to you. You might let your family members get closer to you than you would a stranger. **How do you feel when someone is too close to you?**

It is important to remember that this is the same for other people as well. Whenever you are talking to or interacting with someone, try to keep in mind how close you are to them. It is helpful to read their social clues to see if they are feeling uncomfortable by how close you are to them. If they are turning their body from you or they keep backing away, this might mean that you are in their personal space. It could also mean that they are not interested in the conversation and are trying to send you the message by increasing the space between the two of you.

Touch

Touching others is something that you have to be very careful about doing. Not everyone likes to be touched, even by people who are close to them. It is best to keep your hands to yourself when interacting with other people, especially those you have just met.

 **ACTIVITY**

Personal Space

Answer the questions below about who you feel comfortable letting into your different personal space zones. Which zone do you allow your friends into? What about teachers?

Who is allowed in ① ?

_____

_____

_____

_____

_____

Who is allowed in ② ?

_____

_____

_____

_____

_____

Who is allowed in ③ ?

_____

_____

_____

_____

_____

DISCUSSION QUESTIONS

1. What does it take for someone to be allowed into your Zone 1?

2. What do you do if people in Zone 2 or 3, try to get into Zone 1?

Voice Tone

Sometimes it's not what you say, but *how* you say something that can make all the difference. Your tone of voice can let others know how you're feeling in the moment. You could be saying the exact same sentence, but if you were to change your tone of voice, it would express different meanings. Look at the two examples below.

If you look at the difference in social clues from both boys, you can guess that Boy #1 is feeling sad and Boy #2 is angry. Even though they're both saying the same thing, you can imagine that their tone of voice and body language send a different message.

Sarcasm

Sarcasm is when someone says the opposite of what they really mean. When people use sarcasm, they usually change the tone of their voice. Sarcastic comments can be said jokingly, and other times it can be used to be mean.

For example, if you see your friend trip and fall in the hallway, and you walk up to them and ask, "Hey, how's it going?" If they were being sarcastic, they might reply, "Great! This is the best day ever! Can't you tell?"

If you didn't know that they were being sarcastic, you would be confused. That's why it is important to listen to the tone of voice as well as other social clues.

Volume

Having good social skills also means that you are aware of the volume of your voice at all times. It is important to be mindful of how loudly or how quietly you are communicating with other people depending on the setting you are in. The volume of your voice needs to be adjusted whenever you're having a conversation with someone. The closer you are to them, the lower your voice should be.

Voice volume can also give you clues about how someone might be feeling. If they are speaking softly and quietly, you can guess that they might be shy or sad. If they are yelling and screaming, then they might be mad or excited.

Voice Volume

Indicate how loud the volume of your voice should be at these locations.

Very Quiet		Whisper		Normal Volume		Loud!		As Loud as I Want!	
1	**2**	**3**	**4**	**5**	**6**	**7**	**8**	**9**	**10**

IN THE LIBRARY _____

AT YOUR FRIEND'S HOUSE _____

AT A RESTAURANT _____

IN THE CLASSROOM _____

AT THE PARK _____

IN YOUR HOUSE _____

AT A CONCERT _____

HAVING A CONVERSATION _____

IN THE HALLWAY _____

IN A STORE _____

IN YOUR BACKYARD _____

AT THE DOCTOR'S OFFICE _____

DISCUSSION QUESTIONS

1. What would happen if you were loud in places you're supposed to be quiet?

2. What would happen if you were quiet in places you're allowed to be loud?

Putting it All Together!

When you put social clues all together, you have a better chance of knowing how people are thinking or feeling in the moment. If someone's facial expression suggests that they are upset, you can look at the rest of their social clues to see if it matches up. Are their fists clenched? Are they standing close to you? If their body expresses anger, and they are talking in a stern tone or yelling, then it can be safe to guess that they are feeling angry.

Ask When in Doubt

There are times when it can be hard to guess how someone is feeling by only looking at their social clues. If you ever truly want to know how someone is feeling you can always just ask:

"How are you feeling right now?"

Putting It All Together

Describe the social clues you might expect to see from someone experiencing each of these feelings.

BORED

Facial Expression	Body Language
Space	**Voice Volume and Tone**

Draw a picture of what a bored person might look like!

SCARED

Facial Expression	Body Language
Space	Voice Volume and Tone

Draw a picture of what a scared person might look like!

ANNOYED

Facial Expression	Body Language
Space	Voice Volume and Tone

Draw a picture of what an annoyed person might look like!

DISCUSSION QUESTIONS

1. What are the differences in facial expression and body language you notice with all the feelings?

2. What are the differences in space and voice volume/tone you notice with all the feelings?

Chapter Wrap-Up

What are the four parts that make up social clues?

1. _____

2. _____

3. _____

4. _____

Verbal means using your words to communicate. True or False? _____

The way that you sit or stand is known as your _____.

What is an example of a gesture? _____

What is sarcasm?

_____

_____

True or False? You can be as loud as you want to be, all the time! _____

Being close to someone and making them uncomfortable means that you are invading

their __ __ __ __ __ __ __ __   __ __ __ __ __!

How you say something is known as your voice _____.

If you're ever not sure how someone is feeling, what can you ask them?

" _____ ?"

CHAPTER 3

Talking and Listening

Having a Conversation

A conversation is a great way to get to know more about another person. Good conversations can often lead to friendships. Knowing how to start, maintain, and end a conversation is a very important part of interacting with other people. When people are having a conversation, they like to feel like the other person is listening and is interested in what they have to say.

Starting a conversation can be challenging. Some people feel shy and nervous when they are around other people. Others have a hard time knowing exactly what to say to get a conversation started.

What makes it hard for *you* to start a conversation sometimes?

_____

_____

_____

_____

_____

This chapter will give you tips on how to start, maintain, and end a conversation in a way that makes both you and the other person feel good!

Before You Start...

When starting a conversation, there are a few things you need to consider before approaching the other person.

Here are a few questions you should ask yourself first!

Are they busy or are they available to talk right now?

What's the goal of my conversation?

How are they feeling based on their social clues?

Is this the best time and place to have a conversation?

What am I going to say to start this conversation?

Asking and answering these questions can help you feel more comfortable and prepared when starting conversations with others.

Before You Start...

Are they busy or are they available to talk right now?

Before jumping into any conversation, it is important to first sit back and observe for a bit. You want to figure out if this person is currently busy or not. If they look occupied or distracted, then more than likely, they don't want to be bothered with conversation at the moment.

How are they feeling based on their social clues?

While you're observing, use social clues to see how they might be feeling. Even if they are not busy, they might look like they're in a bad mood. Sometimes it is still helpful to talk to people even if they don't look like they're happy. For instance, if you see your friend with their head down and they are crying, you can use social clues to guess that they are feeling sad. This will help you know what to say to them to start the conversation. It might be helpful to check in and ask how you can help them feel better.

Is this the best time and place to have a conversation?

If you're at a place where you're not supposed to be talking, like a library, it might not be the best place to approach someone for conversation. Also, if you know you don't have a lot of time to carry out the conversation, it might be best to wait for another opportunity.

What's the goal of my conversation?

Having a goal for the conversation can help you determine the direction of the conversation. Is your goal to try to make a new friend, or are you just wanting to share information? Sometimes it is helpful to plan what you are going to say, and this is made easier if you have a goal in mind.

What am I going to say to start this conversation?

This is a hard one! Starting a conversation usually involves asking the other person a question. There are more tips on the next few pages to help you out!

 **ACTIVITY**

Ready for Convo!

Take a look at each person's social clues and answer whether you think they look like they are ready and willing to have a conversation.

Does this person look like they want to have a conversation?   **YES**   **NO**

How can you tell?

_____

How do you think this person is feeling? _____

What might happen if you were to try to have a conversation with them?

_____

_____

Does this person look like they want to have a conversation?   **YES**   **NO**

How can you tell?

_____

How do you think this person is feeling? _____

What might happen if you were to try to have a conversation with them?

_____

_____

Does this person look like they want to have a conversation? **YES** **NO**

How can you tell?

_____

How do you think this person is feeling? _____

What might happen if you were to try to have a conversation with them?

_____

_____

DISCUSSION QUESTIONS

1. Was it difficult to tell which person looked like they were ready for conversation?

2. Can you share about a time when you tried to talk to someone who wasn't ready for conversation?

Tips for Starting a Conversation

1) Using social clues, find the right time to start the conversation.

2) Smile as you are greeting the other person. Make sure that your body language shows that you are warm and friendly.

3) Make an effort to remember their name. If you're not good at remembering names, repeat it back to them when they introduce themselves. *"Nice to meet you, Marie."*

4) Talk about the location, the activity, or the event that you're both attending. *"This is a pretty cool park. Is this your first time coming here?"*

5) Make a comment about something that you observe them doing, and follow it up with a question. *"I see you really like playing with racecars. Which one is your favorite?"*

6) Discuss a current event. This should be something that you think the person might be interested in. *"Hey, did you hear about..."*

7) Ask them a question about themselves. Most people enjoy sharing about their interests with others. This will also help you get to know more about them and hopefully be able to find something that you have in common.

8) Give them a compliment and ask a question to follow it. *"That's a really nice hat! Where did you get it?"*

9) Identify some things that you have in common and point it out to them. *"Looks like we're reading the same book. Have you read the first one in the series?"*

10) Ask them for information related to what you're both doing at the time. If you're in the lunch line, you could ask, *"Hey, do you know how many cookies we're allowed to have?"* You could follow it up with, *"They're really good! Have you had these before?"*

ACTIVITY

Conversation Starters

What are some things each person can say to start a conversation?

It's the first day of school. Jasmine and Priscilla are waiting for the bus to arrive. What do you think Jasmine can say to Priscilla to get the conversation started?

" _____ "

" _____ "

" _____ "

Ken sees Breanna playing basketball by herself. He wants to have a conversation with her and play basketball too. What do you think Ken can say to Breanna to get the conversation started?

" _____ "

" _____ "

" _____ "

Mario and Filip are both waiting in line to see the new movie, *Attack of the Purple Squirrels*. They are both there by themselves. What do you think Mario can say to Filip to get the conversation started?

“ _____ ”

_____

“ _____ ”

_____

“ _____ ”

_____

DISCUSSION QUESTIONS

1. What are some situations where you have trouble starting a conversation?

2. What do you think some good conversation starters would be in those moments?

Looking Approachable

There are times that someone might want to start a conversation with *you*. It is important to make sure that you look **approachable** to others. This means that your facial expression and body language sends a message letting them know that you are ready and willing to have a conversation with them. Below are a few things that you can do to make yourself look approachable and inviting to others so that they feel more confident talking with you.

LOOK AVAILABLE FOR CONVERSATION!

SMILE AND LOOK FRIENDLY!

TURN YOUR BODY TOWARDS THEM!

MAKE GENTLE EYE CONTACT!

KEEP YOUR HEAD UP AND BE CONFIDENT!

DON'T FIDGET OR LOOK TOO DISTRACTED!

WAVE AND LOOK HAPPY TO SEE THEM!

MAKE SURE YOU HAVE GOOD HYGIENE!

Maintaining a Conversation

OK, you did it! You successfully started a conversation. Now what? Keeping a conversation going takes work from both people involved. It requires giving your full attention to the other person and taking turns talking.

But a conversation is not only about talking and knowing what to say. It is also important to learn how to be a good and active listener so that the other person wants to remain in the conversation.

Poor Listening Skills

Everyone wants to leave a conversation feeling like the other person listened to them and was interested in what they were saying. Being a poor listener can make people feel unheard and disrespected. Below are the characteristics of a poor listener.

Poor Listener

* Tries to multitask while talking. **Multitasking** is when you are trying to do many things at the same time. Some people are able to do this well and still listen, but if you're not giving someone your full attention, it can look like you don't care.

* Plans too far ahead what they might say. Being too focused on what you want to say next can keep you from hearing what the other person is saying now.

* Doesn't ask questions about the other person, instead they talk about themselves for most of the conversation.

* Dominates the conversation. Doesn't allow the other person much time to talk.

* Is easily distracted by things going on around them and doesn't give good eye contact.

* Interrupts or makes comments that have nothing to do with the conversation.

* Looks like they are not interested in the conversation because of their body language.

Which of these poor listening behaviors do you do when you are having a conversation?

Active Listening Skills

Have you ever been talking to someone and wondered, "Are they even listening to me?!" You might have felt this way because they weren't *showing* you through their social clues that they were listening to you. **Active listening** means that you are showing others through your body language, facial expression, and words that you are paying attention and are interested in what they have to say. Below are the characteristics of an active listener.

Active Listener

* Gives the other person consistent eye contact as they are speaking.

* Is focused and not distracted. They are giving the speaker their full attention.

* Provides encouragement for the other person to keep talking by saying things such as "go on" and "tell me more".

* Says small things to let the speaker know that they're listening, such as "uh huh" and "I see".

* Matches the speaker's body language. If the speaker appears excited, they become excited as well.

* Does not interrupt. They let the speaker say everything that they need to say.

* Paraphrases. **Paraphrasing** is repeating back to the speaker parts of what they've said so that you can show that you are listening.

* Asks questions and makes comments to show that they're interested and care about the topic.

Which of these active listening behaviors do you do when you are having a conversation?

Active vs. Poor Listening Skills

Write an "**A**" by the active listening skills and a "**P**" by the poor listening skills.

_____ Making good eye contact

_____ Looking interested in the conversation

_____ Covering your ears and saying, "Na na na na na na – I can't hear you!"

_____ Interrupting as they are talking

_____ Staying focused on the conversation

_____ Being distracted by everything going on in the room

_____ Matching the speaker's body language

_____ Making a comment that has nothing to do with the conversation

_____ Smiling and nodding as they are speaking

_____ Slouching in your chair

_____ Remembering what they say and repeating some of it back to them

_____ Yawning and telling them how bored you are

_____ Encouraging them to keep talking

_____ Playing on your phone while they are talking

DISCUSSION QUESTIONS

1. Which of the active listening skills do you do?
2. Which of the poor listening skills do you do?

Asking Questions

Questions help to keep the conversation going by showing the other person that you are interested in what they are talking about. Imagine if you told someone that you got a brand-new puppy and they didn't ask you any questions about it at all! You would think that they didn't care because they weren't wanting to know more. This is why asking questions is important.

There are two different types of questions that you can use during conversation. A **closed question** is a question that can be answered with one word. For example, if you ask someone, "Did you see the new movie yet?" they could respond just by saying "yes" or "no". A closed question is good for getting quick information, but it can make your conversation very short if you use too many of them.

An **open question** is a question that encourages the other person to provide more detail. For example, if you ask "What did you think of the new movie?", the other person would have to use more words to answer. This helps make for a longer conversation!

Adding Comment

Responding with a comment is also something that you can do to help keep the conversation going. When you make a comment, you want to make sure that it is on topic with what the speaker is talking about. Comments are used to relate to the other person and encourage them to continue talking.

"That must have been very difficult."

"That sounds exciting!"

"I would have done the same thing!"

"You must have felt very upset!"

"I can't even imagine what that's like."

 **ACTIVITY**

Asking Questions

Read each comment and try to think of questions you can ask in response to keep the conversation going.

I'M REALLY LOOKING FORWARD TO SPRING BREAK THIS YEAR.

TODAY IS THE WORST DAY EVER!

DISCUSSION QUESTIONS

1. Was it difficult to come up with questions to ask?

2. How do you think the other person would respond to each question that you came up with?

Best Response

Read the sentences and circle the comment or question that would be the best response in the conversation.

1.) "I just got a new video game yesterday!"

(A) "Only nerds play video games."
(B) "Oh, really? What game did you get?"
(C) "Me too! Mine is probably better."
(D) "Who cares?"

2.) "Oh no! I just got a bad grade on my History quiz."

(A) "Really? That's like the easiest class in the world!"
(B) "I'm really sorry to hear that."
(C) "HAHAHAHAHAHA-HA!"
(D) "Wow! You're really not smart."

3.) "Just one more week until school's out!"

(A) "You seem really excited!"
(B) "Why do you hate school so much?"
(C) "Actually, there's six more days. A week has seven days."
(D) "Calm down! It's not a big deal."

4.) "What's your favorite flavor of ice cream?"

(A) "None of your business."
(B) "Ice cream is gross. Anyone who likes ice cream is a loser!"
(C) "That's a dumb question."
(D) "Chocolate! What's yours?"

5.) "Did you watch the football game yesterday?"

(A)   "Do I look like someone who watches football?!"
(B)   "Did you watch the basketball game yesterday?"
(C)   "Yes! It was such a great game!"
(D)   "No. Bye."

6.) "My dog ran away yesterday. I miss her so much."

(A)   "I'm so sorry to hear that. Is there any way I can help?"
(B)   "It was probably trying to get as far away from you as possible!"
(C)   "That's why you should get a cat. Cats don't do that."
(D)   "Big deal. It's just a dog. Get over it!"

7.) "I really like your new shoes! When did you get them?"

(A)   "Stop looking at them!"
(B)   "I don't remember. Can you just leave me alone?"
(C)   "It doesn't matter. They're mine, not yours."
(D)   "Thanks! I got them for my birthday last week."

8.) "I've got two tickets to the concert tomorrow. Do you want to go?"

(A)   "Yes, but not with you."
(B)   "I'd really like to, but I have plans already."
(C)   "What makes you think I want to go to something like that?!"
(D)   "That sounds really, really boring!"

Answer Key
1.) b   2.) b   3.) a   4.) d   5.) c   6.) a   7.) d   8.) b

DISCUSSION QUESTIONS

1. How do you think the other person would react to each response?

2. What are some other Best Responses that you can think of for each one?

Tips for Maintaining a Conversation

1. Actively listen and show the other person that you're interested in what they are saying. Smile, be attentive, and maintain eye contact.

2. Ask them questions about something they've said during the conversation.

3. Don't talk about yourself too much or brag. This can be off-putting and make people want to end the conversation with you.

4. If they ask a question, ask them the same question back after you answer. *"My favorite color is green. What's yours?"*

5. Ask them to tell you more about a topic that they seem excited about. *"That's awesome! Can you tell me more about that?"*

6. Stay focused on the conversation and try not to get distracted. If you need to step away or take care of something else, be sure to say *"excuse me"*.

7. Do not start an argument when they are sharing their opinion, even if you don't agree with what they're saying. Avoid criticizing them for their views. If you disagree, do so kindly.

8. Take turns speaking and do not interrupt them. You also want to make sure that you're not rambling and taking over the conversation.

9. Stay on topic, especially if it's one that they seem interested in.

10. If there is silence, ask them a question about something they mentioned earlier. *"You said before that you like animals. Do you have any pets?"*

Using Humor

Humor helps us connect with people, and laughter often makes us feel happy. Good conversations usually have some humor involved. While we all like to think that we are funny, we have to be careful how we use humor during conversation. When humor is used well, it can lead to shared connections with others. When it is used poorly, it can cause hurt feelings or moments of awkwardness.

Tips for Using Humor

1. Before telling any jokes, make sure that you know the other person's sense of humor. Do you think they'll find the joke funny or is there a chance they might get offended? If anyone is ever offended by a joke you tell, make sure to apologize.

2. Don't use humor to make fun of other people or the person you're talking to. The other person might get upset and want to leave the conversation.

3. Sometimes, it is okay to make a joke about yourself. But if you do it too much, other people might feel sorry for you instead of laughing along.

4. Don't laugh too hard at your own jokes. Let other people determine how funny your joke is.

5. Watch people's social clues after you tell a joke. If it looks like they are genuinely laughing, then that means they think you are funny. If they look uncomfortable, or aren't laughing, it might be better to hold off on telling any more jokes.

Ending a Conversation

Every conversation must and will come to an end. Sometimes it might be that you or the other person has to leave, or other times, one of you may no longer be interested in the conversation. It is helpful to learn the social clues that let you know if someone wants to end a conversation. Below are things they might say or do to suggest that they want to stop talking with you.

Looking annoyed

Looking around, being distracted

Looking at their watch or a clock

Yawning

Not asking questions back to you

Slowly walking away from you

Turning their body away from you

Giving you short, one-word answers

Changing the topic

Remaining silent or looking disinterested

Cutting you off as you're talking

Tips for Ending a Conversation

1. Continue using your active listening skills all the way through the end of the conversation. You don't want the other person to ever think you're losing interest.

2. Tell them that you've enjoyed the conversation. *"It's been nice talking to you! I'm glad that we got a chance to catch up."*

3. Comment or ask when you'll see them next. *"Take care! I'll see you later in math class."* or *"Great chat! When will I see you next?"*

4. Apologize if you have to go and need to cut the conversation short. Give them an explanation. *"Sorry. I don't mean to be rude, but I need to get going. I don't want to be late for my appointment."*

5. Mention something that they said earlier in the conversation. *"I'll see you later. Good luck on your test!"* **or** *"Bye! I hope your dog feels better."*

6. Tell them to have a good day, week, or weekend depending on when you'll see them again.

7. Say *"goodbye"*, *"take care"*, **or** *"see you later"*.

8. If it looks like they want to end the conversation or are losing interest, you can be the one to end it. They may just be trying to be nice and not hurt your feelings. You could say, *"Well, I don't want to keep you much longer. It's been nice talking with you."*

9. Ask for a way to stay in touch with them. *"I need to go right now, but can I get your number so we can chat sometime?"*

10. Make plans with them if they seem interested. *"It's been nice talking with you. We should definitely hang out sometime."* or *"What are you doing on Friday night? Let's make plans!"*

 **ACTIVITY** # Ending a Conversation

Color in the best responses to end a conversation.

I have to leave now because I'm running late.

Great! Now you've made me late for class...thanks!

Are you done talking yet? Bye!

Thanks for the chat! When will I see you again?

That's five minutes of my life I'll never get back. Glad it's over. Bye!

Why are you walking away from me? That's rude!

I've got some other things to do. I'll catch you later!

It looks like you need to go. It's been nice talking with you.

Geez! Can you just stop talking for ONE second?

DISCUSSION QUESTIONS

1. How do you think the other person might respond to each of these conversation enders?
2. Have you ever ended a conversation by saying any of these?

Social Anxiety

Some kids and adults get very nervous or scared when they are around other people or they are out in public. Their heart starts beating faster, they begin to sweat, and they have a lot of negative thoughts running through their head. They believe that others are either judging or making fun of them and this causes them to think badly about themselves. This is known as **social anxiety**.

Sometimes it can be so bad that people with social anxiety prefer not to go out in public or interact with others. Even though they want to make friends, they are too nervous and scared to approach anyone and start a conversation.

Being a little bit nervous or shy is normal for most people, but if you ever think that you are avoiding certain situations because of anxiety, it is helpful to talk to an adult. Getting connected with a counselor can help you learn skills to cope with your fear and anxiety!

Chapter Wrap-Up

What are some things you can do to look more approachable to others?

1. _____

2. _____

3. _____

4. _____

Doing two or more things at the same time is called _____.

True or False? An active listener is easily distracted by things around them. _____

"Did you see the new movie yet?" is an example of a(n) _____ question.

"What did you think of the new movie?" is an example of a(n) _____ question.

What is something you can say to start a conversation with someone in your class?

" _____ "

What are some differences between an active listener and a poor listener?

_____

_____

_____

True or False? "See you later, chump!" is a good way to end a conversation. _____

A good way to keep a conversation going is to ____(circle one)____.

(a) stop talking   (b) only talk about yourself   (c) ask questions   (d) walk away

CHAPTER 4

Interacting with Others

Making and Keeping Friends

If you haven't guessed it by now, this whole book is about learning how to have positive interactions with others. Positive interactions and good conversations can often lead to friendships. People make friends in many different ways! It can be through a common activity or through an introduction from another friend or parent. There are certain steps that need to be taken in order to turn a conversation into a friendship. There are also skills and traits that you'll need to have in order to keep your friendship going.

Sometimes you'll need to interact with other people as a member of a team. People work in teams in order to reach a common goal. Being a good teammate means that you are sharing ideas, being supportive, and using your coping skills whenever you get frustrated.

People want to be friends and teammates with someone who is nice and considerate. This means that using good social skills is extremely important! This chapter will help you explore the qualities that make a good friend and will teach you how to work well with others as a member of a team.

YOUR EXPERIENCE

Answer these questions about your friends!

Friend #1 (Name): _____

How did you become friends? _____

_____

What do you two have in common? _____

_____

What do you like about them? _____

_____

Friend #2 (Name): _____

How did you become friends? _____

_____

What do you two have in common? _____

_____

What do you like about them? _____

_____

Friend #3 (Name): _____

How did you become friends? _____

_____

What do you two have in common? _____

_____

What do you like about them? _____

_____

Friend #4 (Name): _____

How did you become friends? _____

_____

What do you two have in common? _____

_____

What do you like about them? _____

_____

YOUR EXPERIENCE

What are some things that make *you* a good friend to others?

_____

_____

_____

_____

Circle the friendship traits that describe you!

Trustworthy	Good listener	Positive
Honest	Helpful	Kind
Loyal	Thoughtful	Funny
Dependable	Encouraging	Generous
Supportive	Nice	Courageous
Patient	Playful	Confident
Caring	Friendly	Nice

Friendship Skills

Place a check mark next to the ones that describe things a good friend does!

_____ Talks about me behind my back

_____ Listens to me when I'm talking

_____ Shares with me

_____ Cheats whenever we play games

_____ Says nice things about me

_____ Makes fun of the way I look

_____ Lies to me all the time

_____ Stands up for me

_____ Laughs along when other people make fun of me

_____ Helps me when I need it

_____ Never wants to hang out with me

_____ Encourages me to keep trying

_____ Compliments me when I do well

_____ Yells at me when I mess up

_____ Is kind and respectful to me

_____ Helps me feel better when I'm sad or mad

DISCUSSION QUESTIONS

1. Which of these friendship skills do you do?
2. Which skills do your friends do?

Friendship Traits Search

You make and keep friends by displaying these traits. See if you can find them all!

Words can be horizontal, vertical, diagonal, and even backwards!

c	o	u	r	a	g	e	o	u	s
o	h	o	n	e	s	t	g	y	u
n	a	p	n	i	c	e	l	l	p
f	l	d	l	c	i	d	h	a	p
i	j	u	t	a	n	f	t	y	o
d	r	k	f	e	y	i	l	o	r
e	m	b	i	p	e	f	p	l	t
n	s	r	u	n	l	o	u	k	i
t	f	v	t	e	d	e	n	l	v
g	n	i	r	a	c	w	h	q	e

Caring	Kind	Confident
Courageous	Loyal	Nice
Friendly	Helpful	Honest
Patient	Playful	Supportive

DISCUSSION QUESTIONS

1. Why do you think each of these traits is important?
2. What are some other friendship traits that you can think of?

Tips for Making Friends

1. Learn how to introduce yourself properly to others.

2. Be open-minded. Be willing to have a conversation with anyone. You never know who could end up becoming your best friend.

3. Be yourself from the very beginning. You want them to be friends with *you* not someone you're pretending to be.

4. Don't expect to become best friends instantly. It takes time to develop a friendship. Just focus on having one positive interaction at a time.

5. As you're talking to people and getting to know them, try to figure out some things you might have in common with them.

6. Once you've identified things you have common, suggest doing the activity with them. *"We both like football! Want to play sometime?"*

7. Get involved in activities to increase the chances of meeting new people.

8. Say "yes" to safe and fun invitations. Be willing to try something new, even if it's something you're not good at, it can still be fun!

9. Give others a chance to see the positive friendship traits that you have.

10. Stay in touch with them to show that you're interested. If it feels like they are not responding, that might mean they're not interested.

Dealing with Rejection

Unfortunately, no matter how many friendship traits you have, not everyone will want to be your friend. This can leave you feeling rejected, sad, hurt, or even angry. It is important to remember that it doesn't always mean that there is something wrong with you. Sometimes two people just aren't a good match or they don't have a lot of things in common.

Getting rejected can lead to negative thoughts such as "Nobody likes me" or "I'll never have any friends". **What are some positive thoughts that you can have instead if you ever get rejected?**

Being rejected by others can also challenge you to take a look at your social skills. Maybe there are things that you can change about the way you act around other people that will help you make and keep friends.

Peer Pressure

Sometimes people will pretend to be your friend in order to get you to do things that you know are wrong. These kids will act nice to you sometimes, but other times they might threaten you or make fun of you if you don't do as they say. These are not your friends! **Peer pressure** is when someone tries to convince you to do something you may not really want to do.

How do you know if it's peer pressure? Here are a few questions you can ask yourself.

Is this something that will get me in trouble?

Does it feel wrong to me?

Are they name calling me or making me feel guilty?

Will this person stop being my friend if I don't do what they want?

Would I do it if an adult were around?

Have you ever experienced peer pressure before?

 **ACTIVITY**

Is This Peer Pressure?

Read the examples below and decide whether you think it is peer pressure.

Ian tells Neil that he won't be his friend anymore unless he helps him cheat on the science test during class. "Come on. Be a pal!" he says.

Is this Peer Pressure?   YES   NO

Why or why not? _____

_____

Samantha and Temi are playing basketball. Samantha hasn't made a basket yet. Temi says, "Keep trying! I know you can do it!"

Is this Peer Pressure?   YES   NO

Why or why not? _____

_____

Riley and Mateo are at lunch. Riley keeps throwing her grapes at the new kid. She hands Mateo a grape and says, "Don't chicken out on me now. Throw it!"

Is this Peer Pressure?   YES   NO

Why or why not? _____

_____

DISCUSSION QUESTIONS

1. How should each person respond to the peer pressure?

2. What is something you can say to someone who is pressuring you to do something you don't want to?

Working as a Team

Having good social skills also means learning how to get along with others in order to reach a goal. As a member of a team, it is important to be encouraging to others and work through any conflict that might arise. This will make your teammates enjoy playing or working alongside you!

Why do you think teamwork is important?

_____

_____

_____

_____

_____

_____

YOUR EXPERIENCE

What team are you a member of? _____

What role do you play? What do you contribute to the team?

_____

_____

_____

How do you get along with others?

_____

_____

_____

What do you do when you get frustrated?

_____

_____

_____

How do you handle losing or not reaching your goal?

_____

_____

_____

Teamwork

Draw a picture of a time you worked well as a member of a team!

Describe what is happening in this picture:

_____

_____

_____

_____

_____

Draw a picture of a time you *didn't* work well as a member of a team!

Describe what is happening in this picture:

_____

_____

_____

_____

_____

_____

DISCUSSION QUESTIONS

1. What differences do you notice in each picture?

2. What is something you could have done differently in the second picture to improve your teamwork?

Tips for Being a Good Team Member

1. Communicate with your teammates respectfully. If you have ideas about how your team can reach your goal, share it!

2. Use your active listening skills when your teammates are sharing their ideas and opinions. Remember to make comments and ask questions.

3. Know that it's OK not to be the leader. Being a good and supportive follower on a team is equally as important!

4. Be reliable. You should be someone that your team can depend on to do their part of the task.

5. Trust in your teammates to do their part. Don't try to take on anyone else's responsibilities unless they ask for help.

6. Be kind and use manners when you're interacting with teammates. Use the words "please", "thank you", and "excuse me".

7. Compliment others on their strengths rather than talking about their weaknesses or what they're doing wrong.

8. If you need to give criticism, make sure that it is constructive. **Constructive criticism** is when you're giving feedback in a kind way to help someone improve. **Destructive criticism** is when feedback is given in a way that hurts their feelings.

9. Remain positive, even when things aren't going well and you feel like quitting. When a team isn't reaching its goal, it's easy to start having a negative attitude. Negative attitudes usually make things worse for the team. Be someone who motivates and encourages.

10. Learn healthy ways of coping with anger and frustrations. You'll learn more about this in the next chapter!

Being a Sore Loser/Winner

Emotions run high during any competitive event! You could either experience the joy of being a winner or the disappointment of losing. The way that you handle winning or losing can impact how other people feel about you after the competition. Regardless of the outcome, you can still use good social skills to keep from being a **sore winner** or **loser**.

What are some things a sore loser does?

_____

_____

_____

_____

What are some things a sore winner does?

_____

_____

_____

_____

What are some things you can do to better cope with losing a competition?

_____

_____

_____

_____

SORE LOSER

Has trouble dealing with feelings of losing; throws a fit

Name-calls and insults the other team

Says that results are "unfair"

Doesn't congratulate the other team

Doesn't finish the game

Blames their teammates for their loss

Gets angry and frustrated easily

SORE WINNER

Overly celebrates after winning

Makes the other team feel bad about losing by laughing at them or name-calling

Shows off their prize or trophy in front of the other team

Continues to brag and boast for a long time after the game is already over

Doesn't consider how other people are feeling

Both of these make it less likely for people to want to play against you again. A good winner or loser is someone who accepts the outcome of the competition. This is called being a *good sport* or showing good sportsmanship. A good sport is someone who is considerate of people's feelings and makes sure to congratulate others and tell them "good job" after the game. **Are you usually a good sport or are you a sore winner/loser?**

There are some people who enjoy competition so much that it stops being fun playing with them. These people are so competitive that they get extremely angry when they start losing or rub it in your face when they're winning. Being too competitive can make other people not want to do any sort of activity with you, even your friends. Healthy competition is all about having fun whether you win or lose!

Manners

Manners are positive and kind things that we do that make people around us appreciate us more. Below are a few examples. **Which of these do you do?**

- Holding the door open for others

- Being polite by saying "please" and "thank you"

- Asking nicely when you want or need something

- Doing something kind for other people

- Apologizing when you've done something wrong

- Letting other people go first

- Not burping, farting, or picking your nose in front of others

- Not talking with your mouth full of food

- Giving up your seat to people who might need it

- Saying "excuse me" if you want someone's attention

- Saying "excuse me" if you need to get past someone

- Offering to share with others

- Complimenting other people

- Remembering people's names

- Being a good listener and not interrupting when others are talking

- Chewing with your mouth closed

- Congratulating others when they do something well

- Being mindful of how loud you are in a public setting

Chapter Wrap-Up

What are some good friendship traits to have?

_____   _____

_____   _____

_____   _____

What is an example of peer pressure?

_____

_____

What is the difference between constructive and destructive criticism?

_____

_____

True or False? A sore loser congratulates the other team after the game. _____

Which one of these is **NOT** a way to make friends?

(a) Be yourself from the very beginning.

(b) Ask them if they want to see something gross.

(c) Suggest doing a common activity with them.

(d) Get involved in activities.

True or False? Saying "excuse me" is an example of good manners. _____

CHAPTER 5

Handling Conflict

Handling Conflict

Even if you have a good relationship with someone, there may come a time when you disagree on something. This is known as **conflict**. Learning healthy ways to handle the conflict can help keep your friendship intact. Handling conflict poorly can lead to you losing friends and damaging relationships with others.

YOUR EXPERIENCE

On this page, draw a picture of a time when you were angry, upset, or annoyed with someone and you handled it well.

How were you feeling? _____   _____

What did they do to make you feel that way? _____

_____

What did you say or do to them? _____

_____

How did they respond? _____

_____

How did the situation end? _____

_____

On this page, draw a picture of a time when you were angry, upset, or annoyed with someone and you *didn't* handle it well.

How were you feeling? _____   _____

What did they do to make you feel that way? _____

_____

What did you say or do to them? _____

_____

How did they respond? _____

_____

How did the situation end? _____

_____

Coping with Anger

Everyone gets angry. Anger is a natural emotion that we experience when things don't go our way or when someone does something to us that we don't like. If you can learn to cope with your anger in a healthy way, then you have a better chance of dealing with the conflict positively.

Coping with anger in a negative way can damage your relationship with others. If you are someone who has a hard time handling your anger, you will see that others might not like being around you because they have to be extra careful not to make you mad.

What are some things that other people do or say that make you feel angry?

What are some ways that you usually cope with each one?

ACTIVITY   Body Warning Signs

Whenever you start to get frustrated or upset, your body sends you warning signs. It is important to pay attention to these signs so that you know when to start using a coping skill. Color in the body warning signs that happen for you!

⚠ WARNING	⚠ WARNING	⚠ WARNING
I START TO FEEL DIZZY!	SWEATING!	MY CHEST FEELS TIGHT!
I FEEL LIKE CRYING!	I HUFF AND PUFF!	MY WHOLE BODY FEELS HOT!
I GET A HEADACHE!	MY HEART BEATS FASTER!	MY BODY STARTS TO SHAKE!
IT'S HARD TO BREATHE!	I CLENCH MY FISTS!	MY MUSCLES HURT!

DISCUSSION QUESTIONS

1. What are some other body warning signs that happen for you when you get angry?
2. Which warning signs happen first? Which happen last?

Anger Coping Skills

Place a ✚ next to a positive coping skill and a ━ next to a negative one!

_____ Hitting, kicking, biting, or tripping

_____ Talking to an adult about your feelings

_____ Trying to get the other person in trouble

_____ Taking a deep breath before responding

_____ Counting to 10 to calm down

_____ Yelling and screaming

_____ Trying to make everyone else feel angry too

_____ Not letting the other person play with your things

_____ Name-calling and insulting

_____ Letting the other person know how you feel, respectfully

_____ Spreading a rumor about the other person

_____ Walking away to cool down

_____ Saying mean things about the person behind their back

DISCUSSION QUESTIONS

1. Which of the positive coping skills have you used before? How did it work out for you?
2. Which of the negative coping skills have you used before? How did it work out for you?

Being Assertive (I-Feel Statement)

A good way of coping with anger and handling conflict is by being **assertive**. Assertiveness is when you stand up for yourself and let someone know how you feel and what you need from them. It is important to know exactly how you are feeling so that you can express it to others.

You always have the right to tell other people how you feel about what they are doing or have done. This may or may not get them to change. Some people will listen to you and try to make changes, and others might dismiss your feelings. It is good to at least make the first effort to let them know how you feel.

A great way to practice assertiveness is by using an **I-Feel statement**. I-Feel statements are designed to let someone know how you are feeling and to tell them what you need them to do differently. There are four parts to an I-Feel statement:

(1) How you are feeling
(2) The behavior that you would like them to stop
(3) The reason you do not like this behavior
(4) What you would like to see them do differently

I feel (1) **sad** when you (2) **yell and call me names** because (3) **it really hurts my feelings**. I would like for you to please (4) **stop calling me names, and speak to me nicely**.

I-Feel statements don't always have to be said exactly in the format above. The important thing with resolving conflict is to be able to let the other person know how they made you feel. You can change the structure of the I-Feel statement to fit your style and the way that you talk to others.

Practice using I-Feel statements on the next page!

I-Feel Statements

Use the different examples below to complete the I-Feel statements.

Your friend keeps poking you and you don't like it.

I feel (1) _____ when you (2) _____

because (3) _____. I would like for you to please

(4) _____.

A classmate takes your things without asking you first.

I feel (1) _____ when you (2) _____

because (3) _____. I would like for you to please

(4) _____.

Your friend is laughing about you behind your back.

I feel (1) _____ when you (2) _____

because (3) _____. I would like for you to please

(4) _____.

Your sibling keeps interrupting you when you're trying to talk.

I feel (1) _____ when you (2) _____

because (3) _____. I would like for you to please

(4) _____.

DISCUSSION QUESTIONS

1. How do you think the other person would respond to each statement above?
2. Think about a time that you've used an I-Feel statement. What did you say?

Who Said It Best?

Read the options and color in the statements that are the most assertive!

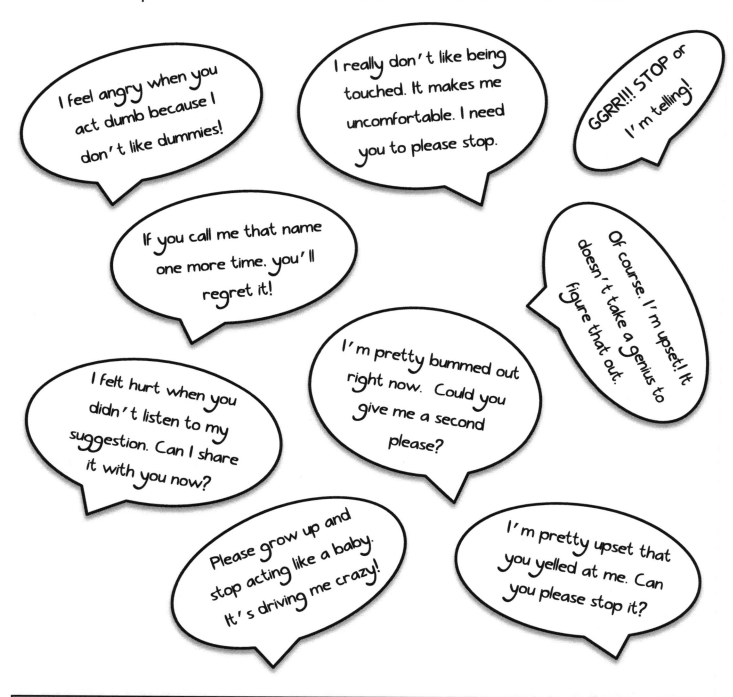

DISCUSSION QUESTIONS

1. How do you think the other person would respond to the ones you colored in?

2. How do you think the other person would respond to the ones that you *didn't* color in?

Other Forms of Communication

Assertive communication is just one of the four forms of communication. It is the best way to get your needs met and resolve conflict quicker. Below are other ways that we communicate with others.

Passive Communication

Passive communication is when you're upset with someone, but you act as if it doesn't bother you and you don't say anything to them. You never let the other person know how you are feeling.

Examples: not saying how you are really feeling, shutting down, laughing and pretending you're not hurt

Aggressive Communication

Aggressive communication is when you use your words, body, or objects to hurt someone else. You're letting them know that you're upset, but it's done in a mean way.

Examples: putting your hands on someone, throwing an object, name-calling, teasing, threatening

Passive-Aggressive Communication

Passive-aggressive communication is when you don't directly tell the other person how you are feeling. Instead you do other things to get back at them and let them know you're upset.

Examples: sulking, giving someone the "cold shoulder", spreading rumors, mumbling under your breath, doing things to secretly annoy them

What is wrong with communicating passively, aggressively, or passive-aggressively?

Forms of Communication

Read each example below and determine which form of communication each person is using.

AG = Aggressive   P = Passive   PA = Passive Aggressive   AS = Assertive

_____ Carlee spreads a rumor about April because she is mad at her.

_____ Eli throws his shoe at Kofi because he's not sharing his toys with him.

_____ Mitchell is mad at Brittani, but he doesn't tell her.

_____ Liam is mad at Greg, so he calls him a mean name.

_____ Jonah tells Nicolas that he hurt his feelings when he made fun of his haircut.

_____ Hannah tells Ursula, "I felt sad when you got on the bus without me."

_____ Mike doesn't tell Fran he's upset because he doesn't want to hurt her feelings.

_____ Rachel ignores Wally all day and won't tell him why she's mad at him.

_____ Hector is mad at Ben, so he knocks his sandwich out of his hands.

_____ Trinity is mad and hides her sister's toy and says, "I have no idea where it is!"

_____ Otis pulls Nia aside and tells her that he needs her to please stop mocking him.

DISCUSSION QUESTIONS

1. When was a time that you handled a situation passively or passive-aggressively?
2. When was a time that you handled a situation aggressively?

Tips for Resolving Conflict

1. Make sure that you are calm. Use your positive coping skills for anger. Try to identify the other feelings that you're experiencing besides anger so that you can express it to that person.

2. Find the right time to confront the person. If you can, try to make it a private conversation when they seem like they are ready to listen.

3. Let the other person know from the beginning that the goal of your discussion is to be able to work things out.

4. Communicate assertively and use an I-Feel statement to express yourself.

5. Allow them the chance to respond to you and share their side of the story. **Agree with the parts of their story that are correct.** *"Yeah, you're right. I did call you a name. I shouldn't have done that."*

6. Actively listen to them and say things to let them know that you are paying attention to what they're saying.

7. Remain respectful throughout the whole conversation. Don't name call or raise your voice. Once you start doing these things, it makes it harder for the other person to want to work things out with you.

8. Be aware that they might not respond the way that you want them to. Many people don't like to be confronted and might become defensive. Stay calm!

9. Apologize for the role that you played in the conflict and be willing to accept their apology and forgive them.

10. Offer a solution or compromise to the problem. A **compromise** is when you and the other person work together to come up with a resolution that you both agree with.

Healthy Conflict Resolution

Read the examples and try to decide the best way to resolve each conflict!

Tucker is on vacation with his family. His parents tell him and his brother that they can pick the next activity for the family to do. Tucker wants to ride bikes on the boardwalk, but his brother says, "No! I want to go to the zoo and see the animals!" What is a healthy way that this conflict can be resolved?

_____

_____

_____

_____

Edie and Constance are in the lunch line. Today the cafeteria is serving pizza rolls, apples, and chocolate cake for dessert. As they get to the end of the line, they notice that there are two pieces of cake left! The kid in front of them takes a slice, leaving only one more. Edie says, "I really want that last piece." Constance does too. What is a healthy way that this conflict can be resolved?

_____

_____

_____

_____

The score is tied at 34 and there are only 2 seconds left in the basketball game. The coach has called a time out and the team huddles together. He asks, "Who wants to take the last shot?" Lonzo and Markelle both say "Me!" at the same time. Only one person will be able to take the shot to win the game. Both boys look at each other angrily. What is a healthy way that this conflict can be resolved?

_____

_____

_____

_____

Darius trades his ninja action figure with Isabel for her toy monster truck. Darius is excited to play with it! When he gets home, he starts playing with the truck and after a little while, he notices that it is broken. Darius is upset and thinks that Isabel gave him a broken toy on purpose. What is a healthy way that this conflict can be resolved?

_____

_____

_____

_____

DISCUSSION QUESTIONS

1. What would be an unhealthy way to handle the conflict in each of the examples?

2. How do you usually resolve conflict with others?

Conflict Comic Strip

Box **1** of the comic strip shows the beginning of the conflict and Box **4** shows the end. Draw and write in boxes 2 and 3 what you think happened for the characters to be able to resolve their conflict in the end!

1. Have any of these examples ever happened to you? How did you resolve the conflict?
2. What would Box 4 look like if the characters handled the conflict in an unhealthy way?

Chapter Wrap-Up

What's an example of a positive coping skill for anger?

_____

What's an example of a negative coping skill for anger?

_____

What are the other forms of communication besides *assertive?*

    1. p __ __ s __ __ __

    2. __ g g __ __ __ __ __ __ __

    3. p __ __ s __ __ __ - __ g g __ __ __ __ __ __ __

What are the four parts of an I-Feel Statement?

    1. _____

    2. _____

    3. _____

    4. _____

True or False? Compromising is a healthy way to handle conflict. _____

What is wrong with this I-Feel Statement? *Hey bird-breath! I feel like hitting you!*

_____

_____

CHAPTER 6

Improving Social Skills

Improving Social Skills

Congratulations! You made it to the last chapter of this workbook. So far, you've learned all about the importance of good social skills when interacting with other people. You've learned how to read social clues, have conversations, work as a member of a team, and handle conflict in a positive way.

This chapter will give you a chance to explore the social skills that you feel *you* need to improve on so that you can have better interactions with your peers and adults.

Identifying Positives

Before we start looking at ways to improve your social skills, let's spend some time talking about the things that you're already doing well! Fill in the circles below.

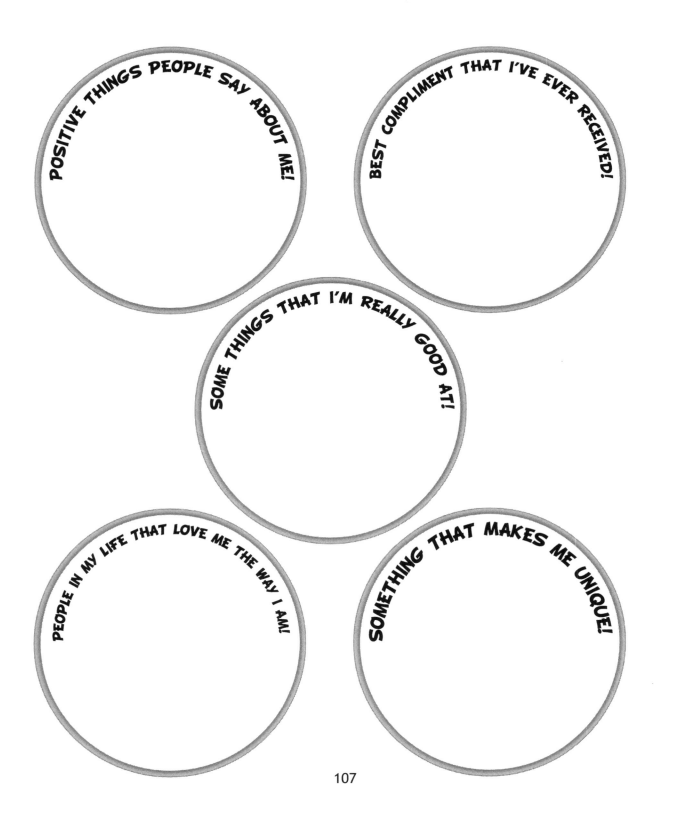

 **ACTIVITY**

Social Skills Checklist

Which skills do you think you need to improve? Place a check mark next to the sentence that is true for you.

_____ I have a hard time understanding how people are thinking or feeling.

_____ I don't work well with other people.

_____ I can't keep friends for a long time.

_____ I get easily distracted when I'm spoken to.

_____ I avoid talking to people because I don't know what to say.

_____ People usually don't laugh at my jokes.

_____ I can be a sore winner or a sore loser sometimes.

_____ I give into peer pressure pretty easily.

_____ I yell and scream, insult people, or throw things whenever I get mad.

_____ I don't understand other people's facial expressions and body language.

_____ People often tell me that I need to _act my age_.

_____ I say inappropriate things sometimes.

_____ I can't keep a conversation going because I don't know what to say.

_____ I rarely say "please", "thank you", or "excuse me".

_____ I invade people's personal space sometimes.

_____ I don't know how to make friends.

_____ I've been told before that I have poor manners.

_____ I get nervous and anxious when I'm around other people.

_____ I don't tell other people how I feel when I'm upset with them.

_____ I have a hard time controlling the volume of my voice.

DISCUSSION QUESTIONS

1. How many of the sentences did you check?

2. Are you ready to do something to start improving your social skills?

Setting Goals

Now that you have identified the social skills that you need to improve, it is time to set some goals! Which of the goals below do you think you need to work on?

☐ I want to get better at reading social clues!

Check this box if you feel that you need to work on learning how to read people's facial expression, body language, and tone/volume of voice.

☐ I want to improve my conversation skills!

Check this box if you feel that you need to work on learning how to start conversations and show people that you are actively listening to them.

☐ I want to learn how to make and keep friends!

Check this box if you feel that you need to work on learning how to make friends and use skills to keep your friendships going.

☐ I want to learn how to better resolve conflict with others!

Check this box if you feel that you need to work on learning how to better cope with your anger and learn ways to communicate assertively with others.

☐ I want to learn how to be a better teammate!

Check this box if you feel that you need to work on learning how to work better as a member of a team and show good sportsmanship whether you win or lose.

What are some other social skills goals that you would like to work on?

1. _____

2. _____

3. _____

The next few pages will give you suggestions to help you reach your goals!

Get Better at Reading Social Clues

Learning how to read social clues takes a lot of practice! Here are a few tips to help you reach your goal:

1. Create a list of common body language movements and facial expressions, and write down what they mean. Get some help from an adult or friend if you have difficulty knowing what a certain social clue means. Study this list often and add to it if you notice a new social clue that you didn't have written down.

2. Watch a TV show or a movie without the volume turned on. See if you can identify how the character is feeling just based off of their social clues. Watch their body language and facial expression to try to guess what they're thinking or feeling.

3. Practice guessing how other people around you are feeling. If you are in a public place, take some time to watch other people's social clues and try to guess how they might be feeling. Think of what might make them feel that way.

4. Play *Feelings Charades* with friends or family. Charades is a game where your partner has to guess the word on the card correctly based on the silent clues that you give them. Write down a feeling word on each card and take turns trying to get the other person to guess just based on social clues. You'll have to pay really close attention to all of the social clues in order to get the answer right!

5. Remember that you're giving off social clues as well. Be mindful of your facial expressions, body language, and voice tone/volume at all times. It can help to practice by looking in the mirror to see how you come across to others.

Improve Conversation Skills

Become more confident starting conversations with others! Here are a few tips to help you reach your goal:

1. Practice your active listening skills with family members. Most people have at least one conversation with a family member each day. Use this conversation to practice your active listening skills, and ask for feedback about how you did.

2. Throughout the day, say to yourself, "If I were to start a conversation with *this* person, what would I say first?" You don't necessarily have to start each conversation, but it is good to work on identifying what you would say if you really wanted to.

3. Think of conversation starters that have worked for you in the past. Always keep a mental list of "go-to" conversation starters that you can use in certain situations.

4. Observe conversations. There's probably someone in your life who does a really good job having conversations with others. It can be helpful to observe this person when they interact with other people to see the things they do to start, maintain, and end conversations.

5. The only way to truly improve your conversation skills is to have more conversations! There are many opportunities during the day for you to be able to strike up a conversation with people around you. Use these moments to practice your skills. After each conversation, try to identify things that you did well and ways that you can still improve.

Make and Keep Friends

Learning and displaying certain skills and traits can help you make and keep friends! Here are a few tips to help you reach your goal:

1. Get involved! The more that you're around different groups of people, the better your chances to meet someone who could be your friend. Joining teams or clubs increases the chances that you'll meet someone with similar interests.

2. Have conversations with different people. Don't limit yourself to a specific type of person. Interact with people that have different backgrounds, ideas, or opinions than you.

3. Practice using good manners. Using good manners increases the chances that people will want to be around you. Ask yourself if there are any behaviors that you do that might annoy others or turn them away. Start changing these behaviors, and you'll notice that people will be more willing to be around you.

4. Use your friendship skills to show the other person that you're glad to have them as a friend. The more that you are kind and respectful to your friends, the closer you'll be. Treat your friends how you want them to treat you.

5. Learn how to stay friends, even after an argument. Most relationships have some sort of conflict, but friendships get stronger if both people are able to learn how to work things out in a healthy way.

6. Do fun things with your friend! It is important that you are participating in activities that you both enjoy doing. This will help to build your bond.

Improve Conflict Resolution Skills

Learning positive conflict resolution skills can help maintain your relationships with others! Here are a few tips to help you reach your goal:

1. Identify positive coping skills that you can use for times when you become upset. Practice using these skills often. In order to successfully resolve conflict with people, you have to make sure that you are calm when you talk to them.

2. Remember that the point of resolving conflict is not to prove that you were right. The goal is to be able to express your feelings and talk about issues without messing up your friendships and relationships.

3. Practice your assertiveness skills with friends and family. The more you practice being assertive, the easier it will be when you need to resolve conflict. You don't have to wait until you're upset to be assertive. Speak up when you have an opinion about certain things rather than staying quiet.

4. It can be helpful to write down your I-Feel statement before you say it. This way, you're able to practice and get comfortable before you confront the other person.

5. It is important to actively listen, even if you're mad at the other person. When listening to their side of the story, try to use empathy to see how they might have been feeling. Doing so will make it easier to come up with solutions.

6. Forgive! Nothing messes up relationships like holding a grudge. If you're both ready to move past the situation, it is important to learn to forgive each other. Do not bring up the issue again when you are mad at the person another time.

Be a Good Team Member

Working well as a member of a team means working together with others to reach a common goal! Here are a few tips to help you reach your goal:

1. Remember that you and your teammates have a common goal. You should play your part to make the team successful, even if that means that you are not a leader. If someone else is the leader, you should be as supportive and helpful as possible.

2. Practice being assertive and sharing your ideas and opinions. A team works best when it gets feedback from all of its members. If you get nervous speaking up in groups, do things that will help calm you down before you share.

3. Learn how to be OK with losing. No matter how good you are at certain things, there will come a time when you will experience losing. It's not a fun feeling, but no matter how you react, you won't be able to change the outcome. It is better to respond in a way that doesn't hurt your relationship with others.

4. If you're someone who gets frustrated easily when working with others, learn how to recognize warning signs that your body sends. For some people, they might start to sweat or their heart might beat faster if they are getting upset. Once you notice these signs, take a step back and use a coping skill in order to calm down.

5. Give positive feedback! Tell others when they've done a good job, even if they were your competition. Pull teammates aside and tell them the things that you notice them doing well. Team members enjoy hearing positive feedback because it helps to keep them motivated.

To continue improving, make sure to get feedback from people you know and trust about what they notice about your social skills. It can be helpful to find a peer or adult who displays good social skills most of the time. You can ask them for help or just observe how they interact positively with others.

You should refer back to the *Social Skills Checklist* on page 106 every few weeks to see if the number of items you check gets smaller and smaller. This will let you know how much progress you're making.

Learning social skills will change a lot of things for the better! Remember to continue to practice these skills whenever you are around other people. Once you start doing these things consistently, you will notice an improvement in your interactions with people in your everyday life!

Workbook Wrap-Up

What are some new things you've learned about social skills that you never knew before?

_____

_____

_____

_____

_____

What can you start doing differently now that you know all about social skills?

_____

_____

_____

_____

_____

_____

_____

_____

Social Skills Crossword

Use the clues from the next page to complete this crossword puzzle!

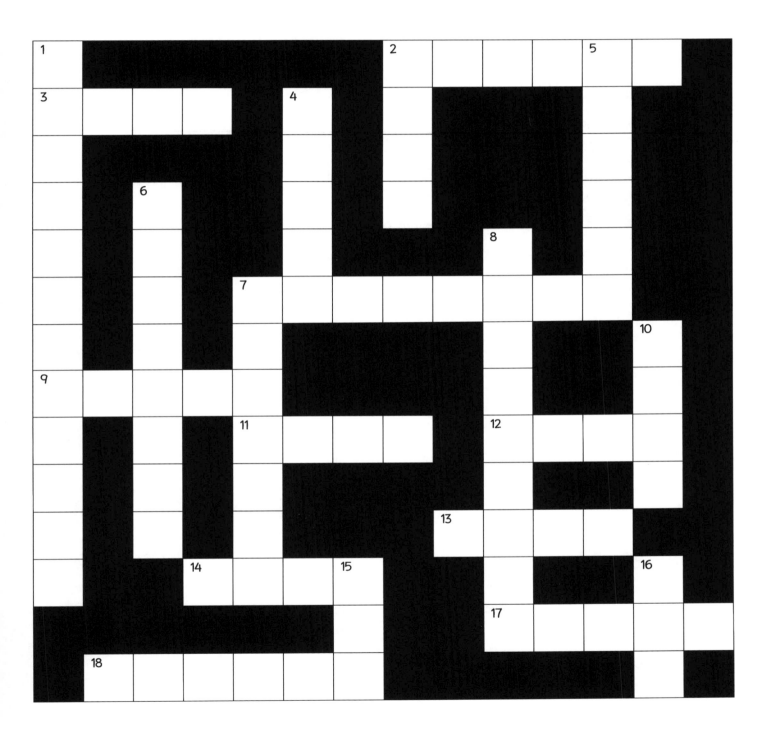

Crossword Clues

Across

2. A _____ expression is when parts of your face move to send a message about how you are feeling.

3. Ask this type of question to make your conversations last longer.

7. Peer _____ is when someone tries to get you to do something you don't want to.

9. Social _____ let us know how other people are thinking or feeling.

11. Being a _____ winner/loser means that you aren't being a good sport.

12. It's not what you say, but *how* you say it.

13. Learning how to deal with your feelings in a healthy way.

14. People you work with to reach a common goal.

17. The distance between two people.

18. Someone who cares about you and supports you.

Down

1. This is criticism that is said in a nice and helpful way.

2. Use an I-_____ statement when you're being assertive with someone.

4. Making people laugh means that you are using _____.

5. _____ listening means that you are *showing* the other person that you are paying attention.

6. Body _____ means that you are communicating using different parts of your body.

7. This type of communication is when you don't express how you are feeling to others.

8. Asking _____ is a great way to keep a conversation going.

10. Taking a _____ breath before responding is an example of a positive coping skill for anger.

15. If a person's fists are clenched and they are scowling, are they happy or mad?

16. "_____ your age!"

ABOUT THE AUTHOR

Z. Andrew Jatau, MS, has served diverse populations in his roles as a case manager, professional counselor, and adjunct professor. He has developed programs and presentations focused on helping children, teens, and young adults develop socially and emotionally. He is the founder and CEO of Mylemarks LLC.

FOR MORE HELPFUL SOCIAL-EMOTIONAL RESOURCES AND TOOLS, VISIT WWW.MYLEMARKS.COM!

Made in the USA
Middletown, DE
25 November 2019